FUTURE SOUNDS

A Book of Contemporary Drumset Concepts

DAVID GARIBALDI

Alfred

DAVID GARIBALDI

Born and raised in the San Francisco Bay area, David began playing drums in elementary school at the age of ten. At age seventeen, he started his professional career, and in 1966 joined the 724th United States Air Force Band. After leaving the service, David joined the legendary Tower of Power band in 1970, of which he was a member for the next ten years. It was in this setting that David became one of the most influential drummers of his generation.

Since 1977, David has appeared in a variety of studio and live settings performing and/or recording with such artists as Patti Austin, Natalie Cole, Larry Carlton, Mickey Hart's Mystery Box, Jermaine Jackson, Ray Obiedo, the Buddy Rich Orchestra, Boz Scaggs, Gino Vannelli, Deniece Williams (band leader for two years), The Yellowjackets, UZEB's bassist Alain Caron, the BBC Orchestra, well-known Japanese producer Mickie Yoshino, pop vocalist Naoko Kawai and the jazz fusion group Wishful Thinking.

Internationally, David performed at the Frankfurt Music Fair in Frankfurt, Germany; the International Drummer's Meeting and International Percussion Day in Koblenz, Germany; Yamaha Big Drummers Camp in Nemo No Sato, Japan; Drum EST '94 in Montréal, Canada; Ultimate Drummers Day in Melbourne, Australia; and Drums in the Bush in London, England. In 1991 and 1994, David was featured at the Modern Drummer Festival in Montclair, New Jersey.

From 1980 through 1985, David won the *Modern Drummer* Reader's Poll "R&B/Funk" category. His name now permanently resides in that poll's honor roll category for his lasting contributions to the percussive arts.

In the field of education, David is very active. From 1982 to 1989 he was on the percussion faculty at the Dick Grove School of Music, taught in the applied music program at California State University, Northridge, and gave seminars at the Percussion Institute of Technology. As his time permits, he teaches at Drum World in San Francisco and is a clinician for Yamaha Drums, Sabian Cymbals, Latin Percussion and Vic Firth Sticks.

As an author, David has written numerous articles for various percussion magazines worldwide, including *Modern Drummer*. His instructional books include *Future Sounds* (Alfred Publishing), which was rated one of the 10 greatest drum books by *Modern Drummer* magazine (Aug. 1993); and *The Funky Beat* (Manhattan Music). David's videos include *Tower of Groove, Parts 1 & 2* and *David Garibaldi featuring Talking Drums*. He is currently working on an instructional book with Talking Drums, a drum ensemble that fuses Afro-Cuban and funk rhythms, plus a solo recording.

David continues to perform, record and teach worldwide. He is presently touring with Mickey Hart's Mystery Box and Talking Drums.

And the beat goes on.

Project Editors:
Sandy Feldstein and Dave Black

CONTENTS

INTRODUCTION

"Future Sounds" is a presentation of ideas for the drum set that is applicable to, and inspired by, contemporary music. The main objective of this work is to help the aspiring drummer in the lengthy process of becoming an individual with a unique, original drum-set vocabulary. This material evolved from my personal playing and study time, coupled with a desire to see my ideas implemented in the musical situations that I've participated in over the years. All of these studies are in the funk/jazz-fusion category and combine technique with a musical idea, an approach further elaborated upon in the opening remarks of the section titled "Groove Studies." To get the most out of the exercises, you must focus on how they are constructed as well as how they are played, so when building your own vocabulary you'll understand how to put your ideas together. A big key in my development over the years has been the writing out of my ideas (which is where all of the exercises contained in this book come from). This has allowed me to see what I'm playing. Through the process of playing and then writing it down, I became much more organized, which greatly improved my ability to make music. I'd first like to stress the importance of having well-developed basic skills—reading, hand technique, rudiments, etc. In other words, the goal is just good overall musicianship. If the foundation of your playing is solid, then you can build whatever you like upon that and it will endure. Exposure to experience is another great building block—playing as often as possible in a variety of settings. Learning to play many styles is what builds depth into your playing regardless of what your favorite style is.

One reason good players become great is that at some point in their development they began to focus on what *they* wanted to express musically instead of continuing to copy their favorite players. Ideally, through lots of playing, practicing, thinking things through, listening, exchanging ideas with others and experimentation, the player will have developed a style and sound of his or her own, as well as many musical ideas. The person then has the option of taking the time to express those ideas, or of choosing to continue to focus mainly on what other drummers are playing, never tapping into the tremendous reservoir of potential within him or herself. Hopefully this book will further open contemporary drumming and will assist you in reaching your goal of being the best player you can possibly be.

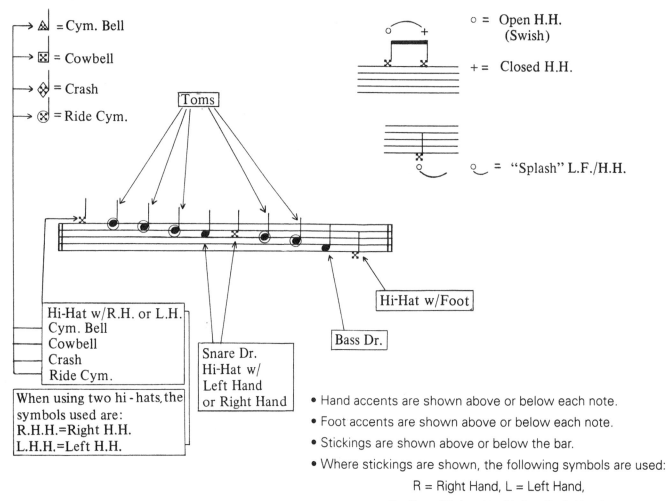

- Hand accents are shown above or below each note.
- Foot accents are shown above or below each note.
- Stickings are shown above or below the bar.
- Where stickings are shown, the following symbols are used:

  R = Right Hand, L = Left Hand,

  F = Foot (Right or Left), B = Both Hands

CONTEMPORARY DRUM-SET PLAYING
Development of Two Sound Levels

There are three basic sounds in contemporary drum-set playing: 1. snare drum (S.D.) 2. bass drum (B.D.) 3. hi-hat (H.H.) In a contemporary music setting, these drum-set components require the most attention because most drum-set music is based on these sounds. Most of the material in the book is written for S.D., B.D. and H.H., with the occasional addition of cym. bell (C.B.), ride cym. (R.C.), cowbell (C.B.) and tom-tom (T.T.) These sounds will expand the tonal possibilities of each exercise. To produce the type of drum-set sounds heard throughout today's music, you must develop two sound levels: accents and non-accents. In a playing situation there will be more than two sound levels, but for our purpose (building foundational drum-set technique) we will be using only two levels. The two sound-level technique gives you a place to begin building a consistent approach to striking the playing surfaces. It not only deals with what is played, but the way in which the playing surfaces are struck and where they are struck, so that your drum sound is compatible with contemporary music. You will find this technique widely used among the top players of the day. The following guidelines will help you develop two sound-level playing.

1. Accents should be played approximately 8"–12" from the playing surface, and non-accents should be played approximately 1/2" from the playing surface.

2. Blend the sounds of the hi-hat and snare drum on the unaccented notes. The snare drum must be played lightly so that it sounds like the hi-hat.

3. The difference in volume between the two levels should be the same as forte (f) to pianissimo (pp). The overall volume will be controlled by the dynamic level of each performance situation, while the relative distance between the two levels of playing will remain more or less the same.

Here are some specific ideas that will help you develop two-level playing on each instrument within your drum set.

SNARE DRUM
Accents—Use rimshots for live playing and some studio situations.

Strike the center of the snare drum with either end of the stick (the butt-end of the stick can thicken the snare drum sound) while the shaft simultaneously strikes the rim between two lugs. This technique produces a slightly lower and thicker snare drum sound.

Non-Accents—Play as an extremely soft, light tap near the center of the snare drum.

To do this, all tension must be released except for the amount required to hold the stick while playing a light tap.

HI-HAT (played with the stick)
Accents—Strike the edge of the hi-hat with the shoulder of the stick.

Non-Accents—Strike the top of the hi-hat (not to be confused with the bell) with the *tip* of the stick.

BASS DRUM
The two-level concept isn't as critical with the feet because most of the time the bass drum is playing notes that require accents. The distance between the sound levels in the feet is less than with the hands [forte (f) to mezzo-forte (mf), or forte (f) to mezzo-piano (mp)]. In any case, the bass drum must be blended with the hands in order to balance all of the sounds properly. The same rules apply when playing the hi-hat with the foot.

RIDE CYMBAL

Playing on the bow
Accents—Ride the cymbal approximately 2" to 2-1/2" below the bell. This produces a more controlled "ping" sound and will help avoid crashing the cymbal each time an accent is required. The cymbal must be played lightly enough in order to avoid sound "buildup."

Also, instead of playing 8" from the surface, go down to approximately 5."

Non-Accents - Play 1/2" above the playing surface as described before.

Playing on the bell
The stick heights are the same as described above for the ride cymbal.

Accents—Strike the bell with the shoulder of the stick.

Non-Accents—Strike the bell with the tip of the stick.

THE TWO SOUND-LEVEL CONCEPT REVIEWED

The "thick" sounds in the "Two Sound-Level Concept" combine:

- B.D. accents
- S.D. rimshots/accents
- H.H. accents w/shoulder of stick
- H.H. played w/foot accents
- R.C. accents with shoulder of stick on bell, tip or bow
- T.T. accents (no rimshot)

The "thin" sounds in a "Two Sound-Level Concept" combine:

- S.D. non-accents (tapping drum lightly)
- H.H. non-accents w/tip of stick
- R.C. non-accents w/tip of stick on bell and on bow
- B.D. non-accents
- H.H. w/foot
- T.T. non-accents

BALANCING THE TWO SOUND LEVELS

Balancing the two sound levels is very important. As was stated before, there are three basic sounds in contemporary drum-set playing. When balancing these three sounds, it's wise to know how drums are mixed on recordings. You can then try to copy that mix when you play. On many of today's records, the snare drum is almost as loud as the lead vocal whereas 15 years ago, the drums were much further back in the mix.

Today the drums are quite up-front in music, so be aware that "loud" drums are not necessarily out-of-place. This changes from year to year, so watch and listen carefully in order to stay on top of these current trends, then adjust accordingly. I'm *not* saying that the drums should be loud to the point of being out-of-place, but loud enough so as to blend in properly with the style of music being performed. Keeping this in mind, when balancing the S.D., B.D. and H.H., the S.D. accent will be the loudest. Next will be the B.D. accent, which is slightly softer than the H.H. accent. It is a more transparent sound, tying the S.D. and B.D. together.

All of the aforementioned techniques are to be applied to every study in this book. Refer to these guidelines as much as possible until they are assimilated into your playing.

When applied properly, the use of the "Two Sound-Level Concept" will give each exercise a musical quality. Read and re-read this section until a thorough understanding of these techniques becomes "your own."

DEVELOPMENT OF THE TWO SOUND LEVELS WITH THE HANDS

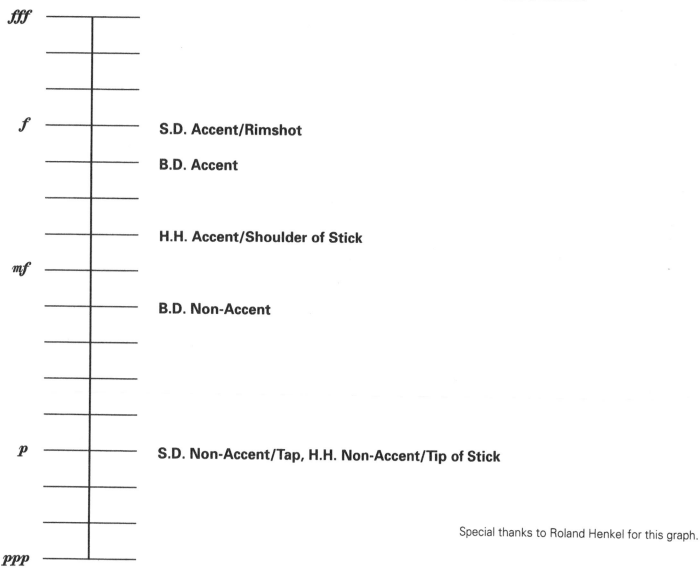

fff

f — S.D. Accent/Rimshot

B.D. Accent

H.H. Accent/Shoulder of Stick

mf

B.D. Non-Accent

p — S.D. Non-Accent/Tap, H.H. Non-Accent/Tip of Stick

Special thanks to Roland Henkel for this graph.

ppp

These levels are always controlled by the dynamic level of the music being played.

I'd like to make one more point before we get into the body of the book.

Rhythm without accents is much like speech that is monotone and lifeless. As an example, let's take the single paradiddle:

This bar contains no accents and, as written, would be played at *one* dynamic level.

This bar, played using the two sound-level concept, sounds much different. Play them both and listen to the difference in the sound and musical feeling.

Once the guidelines are understood, begin working the material in this book. Section #1 is based mostly on paradiddles and is designed to make you feel comfortable applying the two sound levels. While practicing, refer back to this section often.

THE SINGLE PARADIDDLE AND THE INVERTED SINGLE PARADIDDLE AS EIGHTH NOTES

The following 12 exercises are based upon the single paradiddle as eighth notes. In exercises 1–4, the sticking and accents move to the right by one eighth note in each exercise. In exercises 5–8 the sticking remains the same but the accents move to the right by one eighth note in each exercise. Exercises 9–12 are inverted single paradiddles (the double or "diddle" is in the front and is followed by two single accents). The sticking and accents move to the right by one eighth note in each exercise. All 12 exercises are played over a quarter-note bass drum pattern.

The idea of shifting notes and accents is called permutation. Permutation is a mathematical concept and is used frequently throughout this book to expand the rhythmic possibilities of many of the exercises. For a detailed explanation of permutation, see "Permutation Studies," beginning on page 21. By moving the last note of an exercise to the front of the exercise, all other notes are then moved to the right and a different pattern is the result. The last note of each exercise becomes beat one of the *next* exercise and so on (compare exercises 1 and 2 on pages 22 and 23). In a single bar of 4/4 time there are eight eighth notes. By permutating each exercise in the aforementioned manner, eight different patterns will present themselves before coming back to where the permutation process began. If the permutation is done by sixteenth notes, there will be 16 different patterns. If the permutation is done with eighth-note triplets, there will be 12 different patterns. Also keep in mind that the time signature will affect the number of times an exercise can be permutated. If the exercise is in 3/4 and the permutation is done by sixteenths, there will be 12 different patterns. This system works for any pattern, fill or solo idea and can be very helpful in developing a rhythmic/drum-set vocabulary.

The single bar at the top of the exercises is a time pattern that is to be played before each exercise. Play four bars of time and then the written exercise for four bars. The exercises can be performed in sequence or randomly. The idea is to have continuous playing from top to bottom, going back and forth from the time pattern to each written exercise. The tempo for these exercises is ($\downarrow$ = 144) but can be played much slower. Playing each exercise slowly at first ($\downarrow$ = 72) is excellent for building control. Once the material is learned and can be performed comfortably and accurately, begin advancing the tempo.

DEVELOPING THE TWO SOUND-LEVEL CONCEPT
The Single Paradiddle as Eighth Notes

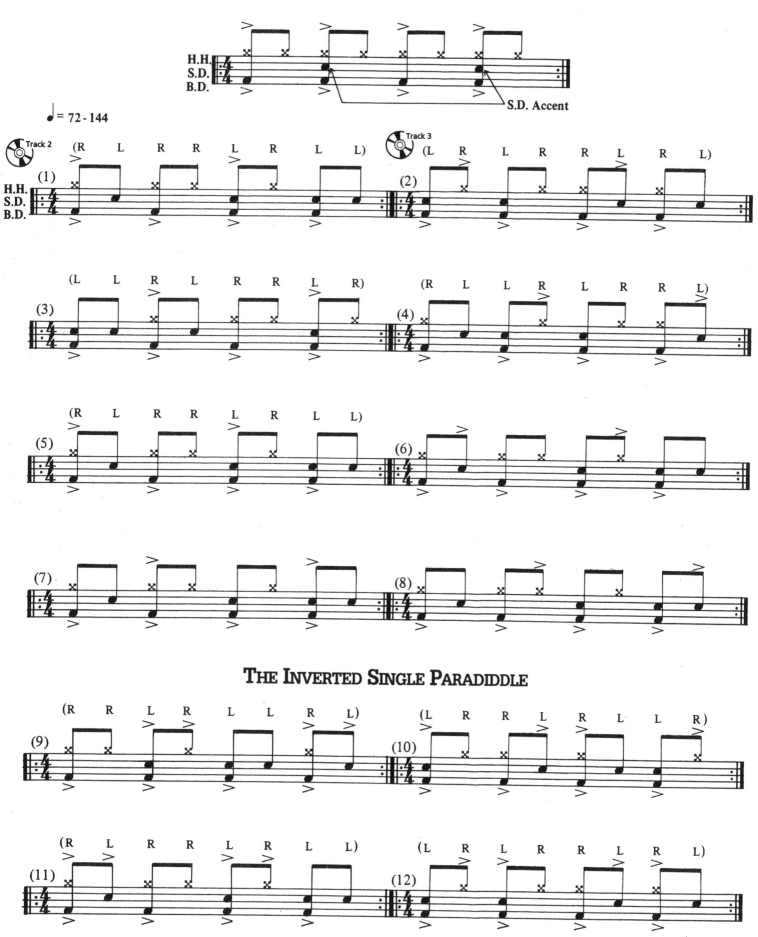

THE INVERTED SINGLE PARADIDDLE

THE SINGLE PARADIDDLE AND THE INVERTED SINGLE PARADIDDLE AS EIGHTH-NOTE TRIPLETS

These eight exercises are a little different than the previous eighth- and sixteenth-note studies. This sticking takes two bars to complete because the triplet is a three-note rhythm and the single paradiddle is a four-note sticking. Exercises 1–4 are single paradiddles that permutate to the right by one eighth note in each exercise. Exercises 5–8 are inverted single paradiddles that permutate to the right by one eighth note in each exercise. There are two time patterns, (A) and (B)—either one can be used (also keep in mind that any time pattern will work). Play four bars of time, then four bars of the written exercise (one repeat).

‖: Four bars time ‖: Four bars exercise (one repeat) :‖

... or work each exercise individually. (See practice tip on page 19.)

THE SINGLE PARADIDDLE AS EIGHTH-NOTE TRIPLETS

Time Pattern:

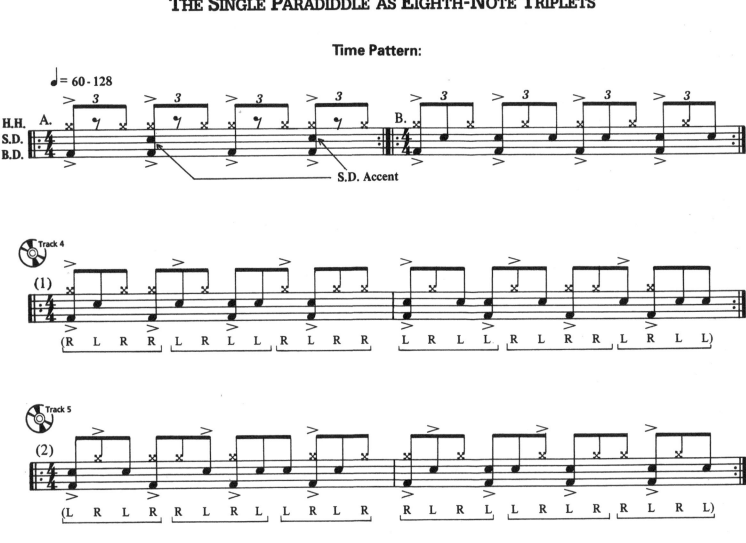

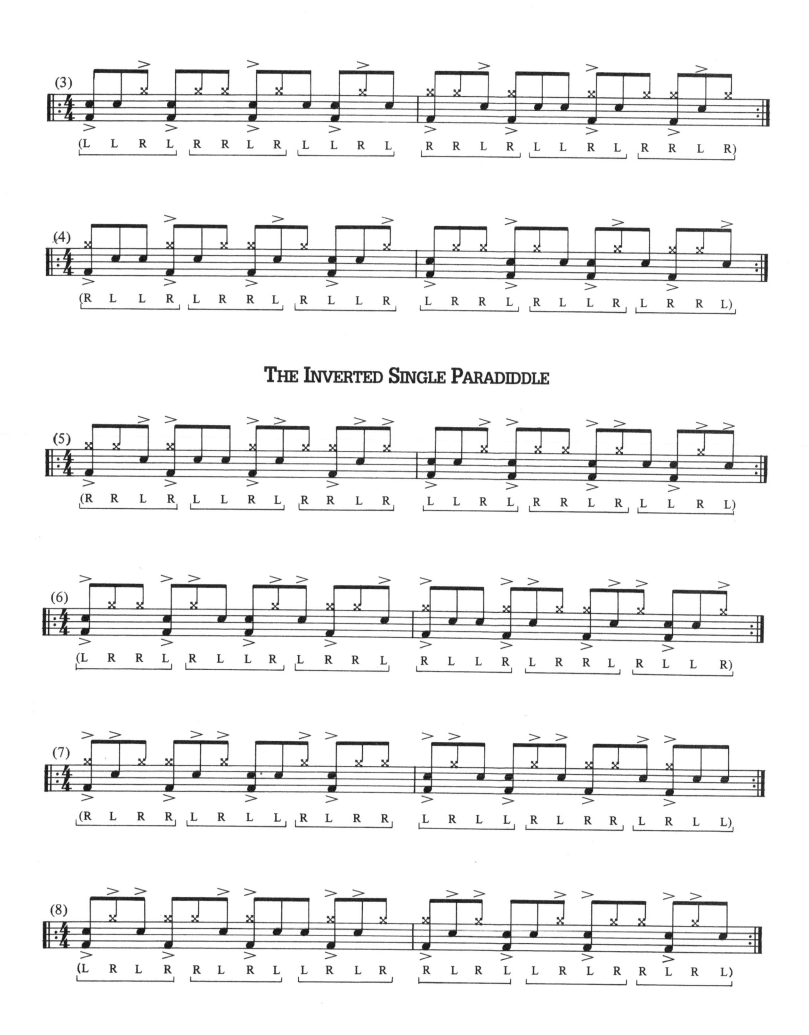

THE INVERTED SINGLE PARADIDDLE

THE SINGLE PARADIDDLE AND THE INVERTED SINGLE PARADIDDLE AS SIXTEENTH NOTES

The idea here is basically the same as in the previous eighth-note exercises, except with sixteenth notes. In exercises 1–4, the sticking and accents permutate to the right one sixteenth note in each exercise. In exercises 5–8, the sticking stays the same and the accents permutate to the right one sixteenth note in each exercise. In exercises 9–12, the sticking and accents permutate to the right one sixteenth note in each exercise. The bar at the top of the exercises is the time pattern to be played in front of each exercise. Play four or eight bars of time, then play four or eight bars of a written exercise. Begin at ♩ = 72 or whatever tempo is desired.

‖: Four or eight bars time :‖: Four or eight bars exercise :‖

Practice tip:

Begin by playing only the B.D. part. As you are playing the B.D. part, play the first four or five notes with the hands until they are performed accurately with the correct accents and non-accents. Next, begin adding one or two notes until the pattern is complete. For a more detailed explanation and further practice suggestions, see page 40 ("Groove Studies").

Time Pattern:

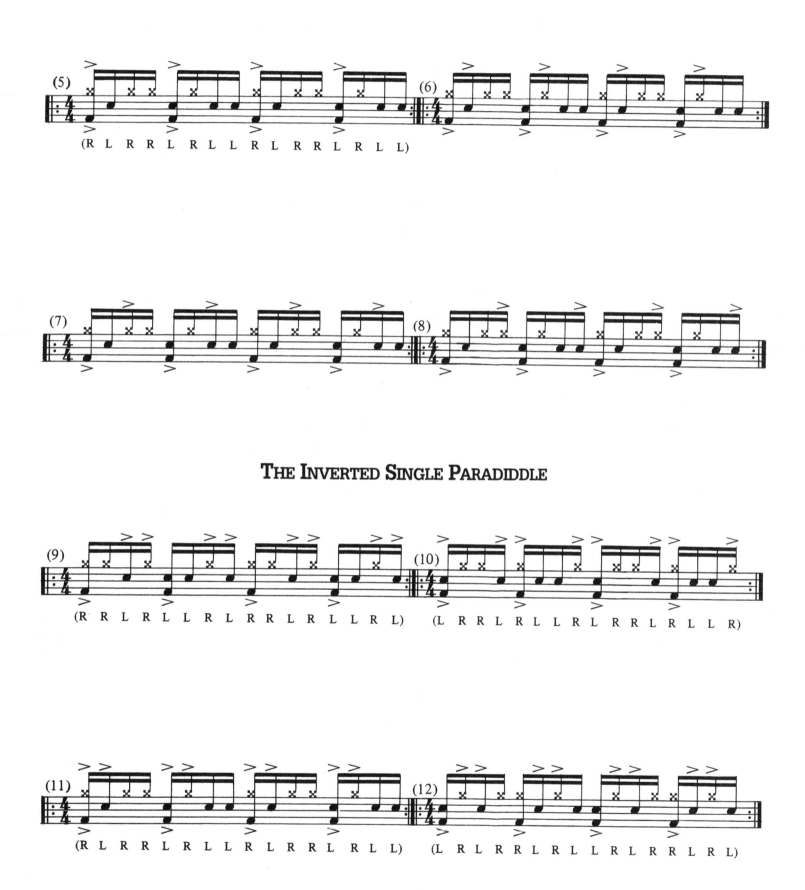

THE INVERTED SINGLE PARADIDDLE

14

FOUR-BAR PATTERNS

Exercises 1–14 are patterns that take four bars to complete. Each bar within each numbered exercise is lettered so you can work them individually.

Exercises 1–5 use a four-bar S.D. and B.D. pattern that turns around backwards in measures 3 and 4, while the H.H. plays a one-bar pattern.

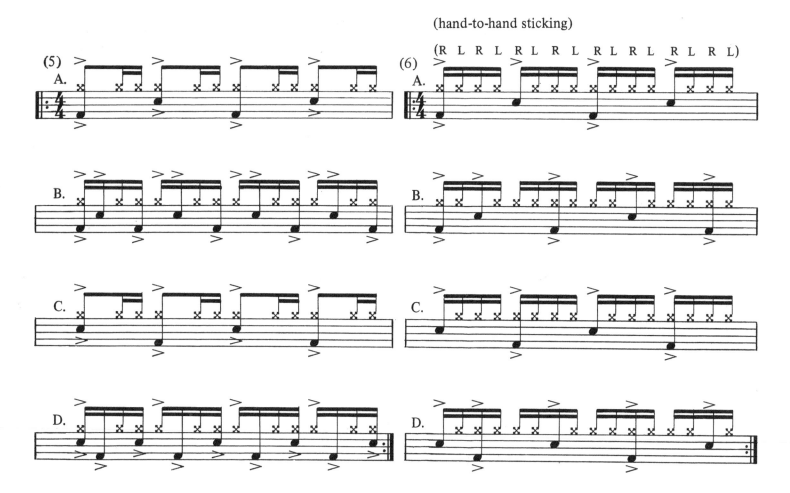

(hand-to-hand sticking)

(R L R L R L R L R L R L R L R L)

Exercises 7–10 are much the same as exercises 1–5 except the R.H. plays the cymbal bell and the L.F. plays eighth notes with the H.H.

Accent all S.D. and B.D. in exercises 7–12.

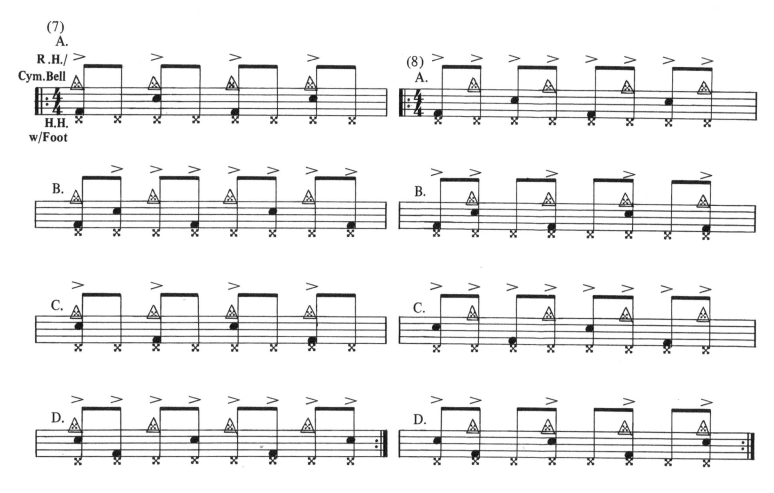

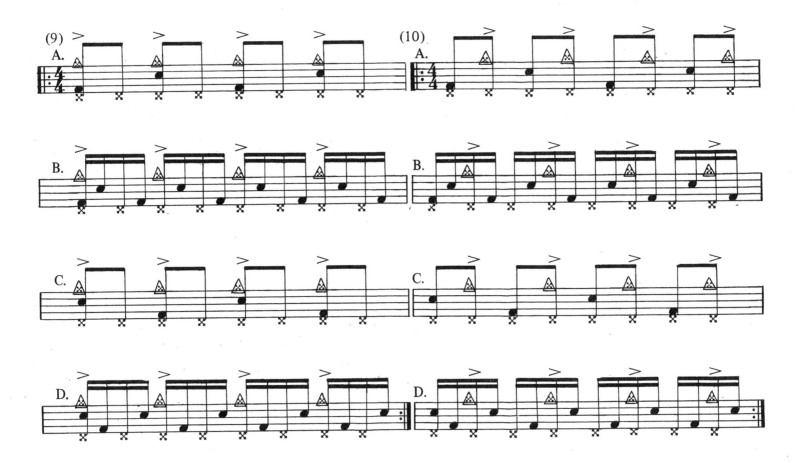

Exercises 11–12 use the ride cymbal instead of the cymbal bell.

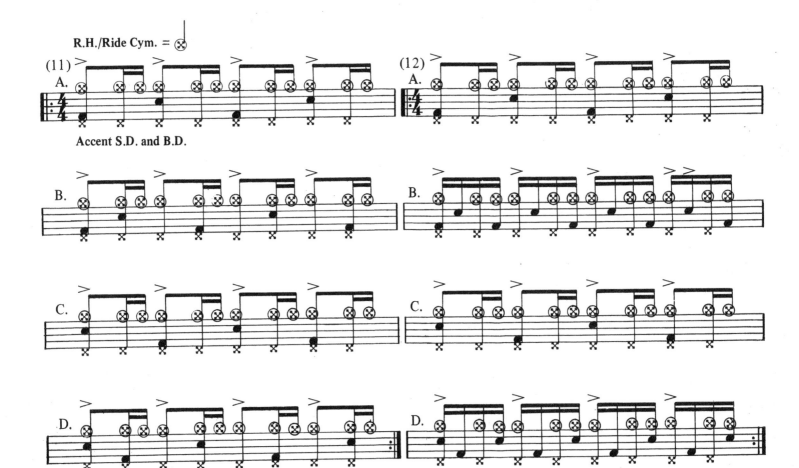

In exercise 13 the H.H. and S.D. are played with the L.H. while the R.F. plays quarter notes with the B.D. The R.H. plays a four-bar pattern with the cymbal bell.

In exercise 14 the L.H. plays the H.H. and S.D. while a four-bar pattern is played by the R.H./cymbal bell and R.F./B.D.

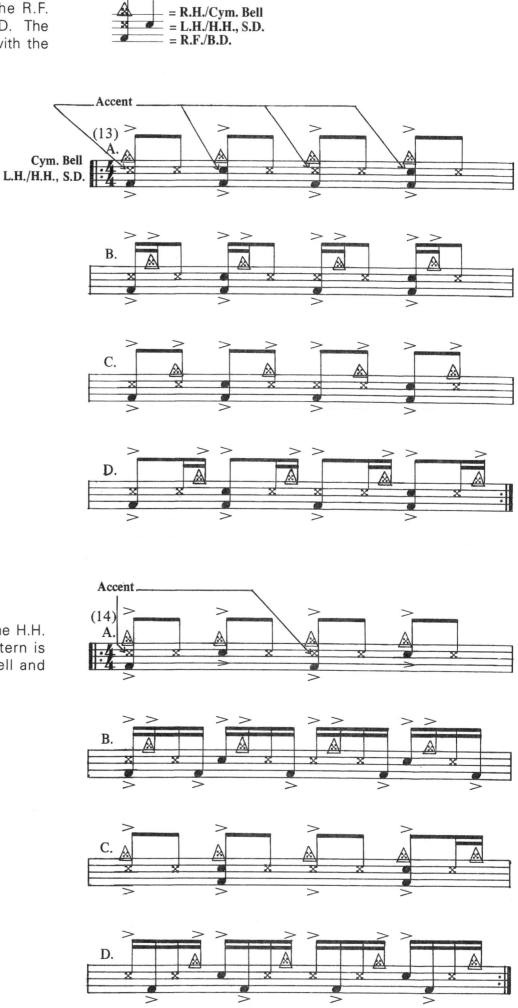

GROOVE PLAYING

Laying down a solid groove is by far the most important element of contemporary drum-set playing. Whether it be a simple pattern or a complex pattern, there must be a groove no matter what the tempo is. If you were to sit down and listen to all the great groove players in contemporary music (though they may differ stylistically), the way each performs within the framework of the time will be very much the same—a machine-like consistency from beat to beat and from section to section within a tune. Although there will be a whole section of groove studies later in this book, the concept is essential in all of this material.

The way in which the time is perceived is very important and can definitely be learned as well as improved upon. Ed Soph, a great drummer and teacher, says that "even time-keeping" is produced by strokes and silence *in time*. The silences or rests between strokes must be perceived evenly, as well as the strokes that are being played. This can be likened to ear training—learning to perceive the intervals between notes so that these intervals can be randomly performed, the goal being the ability to play time with machine-like precision and consistency. Working with a drum machine or click can be of great benefit in this process. Playing patterns at various tempos until they groove is a tedious but rewarding exercise. Taping yourself so you can hear any timing errors is also very helpful. Concentration plays a big part in this and very often timing errors are due to lack of concentration. Good mental focus will minimize those types of mistakes.

You will continue on your "quest for the more perfect groove" by further applying those previously mentioned basics in a series of hand/foot exercises.

Here are some practice suggestions:

• Use a click or a drum machine to play along with.

• Make sure each exercise is played very slowly at first. This will help in building control. Begin at ♩ = 60, then advance the tempo gradually until all metronome markings within the tempo range can be performed accurately.

• Play each exercise for five minutes without stopping, maintaining a controlled, even groove. While playing, focus on each limb and relax, remembering that tension inhibits execution.

• Without playing a note, mentally picture what each limb is to do, making sure you know what each individual part does and how they fit together as a whole pattern. Do this often, because if you can't picture yourself playing these grooves, accomplishment becomes very difficult. This is one of the most important keys in the development of hand/foot coordination. If you are having a problem with coordinating your hands and feet, a great thing to remember is that coordination is basically organization. The more organized one is regarding the interaction of mind, hands and feet, the easier it becomes to coordinate them when making music.

Practice each exercise as written, paying close attention to the accented and unaccented notes. Learning the rhythms or stickings first, then adding the accents later is extra, unnecessary work. Retraining yourself to play the accents and non-accents is added work that can be avoided by playing them correctly from the start. Should this process be too difficult at first, it can be eased somewhat by taking the first three or four notes of a pattern (or any number of notes you're comfortable with) and playing them over and over until they are performed correctly. Then add one or two notes at a time until the entire pattern can be performed as written. All of this should be practiced to a click or drum machine (see exercises 1A–1G on pages 19 and 20).

PRACTICING AN EXERCISE

First, pick an exercise you would like to play.

Next, set your drum machine or metronome to the desired tempo.

While the click is running, play the first three notes—count *aloud* while you do this.

Repeat this measure over and over, making sure that all the accented notes are loud enough, that all the unaccented notes are light enough and that you're playing the time evenly. When you can perform this much perfectly, add the next note.

Continue this process until you've added all the notes. Remember to get into the habit of counting aloud—this is an excellent way of unifying the mind, hands and feet.

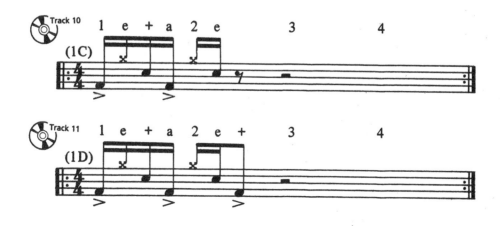

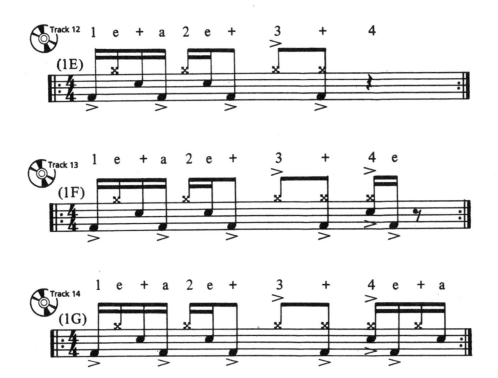

Using this method of progressively adding notes will allow you to work through any exercise in this book, as well as any other material you may be working on. This technique is especially helpful in developing control over the unaccented notes.

When playing exercises that have an eighth-note or quarter-note H.H. pattern, use the H.H. like you would a click. Start first with the H.H. pattern, then progressively add the S.D. and B.D. parts one or two notes at a time until you can play the entire H.H., S.D., B.D. combination. The same is true for the exercises that use a quarter-note B.D. pattern. Use the B.D. as a click, then progressively add the hand parts.

FUNK DRUMMING

Funk drumming is best described as great groove playing plus innovative hand/foot combinations. This style is basically generated from the H.H., S.D. and B.D. voices of the drum set and includes, but is not limited to, playing 2 and 4 on the S.D. In the funk style, any hand/foot combination will work as long as it has a strong groove and fits with the music.

Jazz-fusion drumming and funk drumming are very closely related. Both are very sixteenth-note oriented, both (at times) draw upon various ethnic music for content, both require a very strong groove sense and both can be very improvisational.

PERMUTATION STUDIES

Permutation is a mathematical term defined as "any of the total number of groupings possible within a group." For example, take the sequence 1–2–3–4. If this sequence were to be permutated by one number, the result would be 4–1–2–3 or 3–4–1–2 or 2–3–4–1. As can be clearly seen by this example, the next permutation of the sequence 2–3–4–1 would be 1–2–3–4, which takes us back to the beginning. Because rhythm is mathematical, the variety encountered is endless. Applying this permutation concept to rhythm opens up a very large area of study and can be extremely helpful in the building of one's drum-set vocabulary. To apply this concept, begin with any time signature. Let's examine 4/4, for example. The top number is the number of counts or beats per measure (4), the bottom number is the type of note that gets one count or beat (4, a quarter note). There are four sixteenth notes per quarter note. In a measure of 4/4 there are four quarter notes equaling 16 sixteenth notes. Now, to apply the permutation concept, begin with permutation study #1, exercise 1. In this study the hands play simple eighth-note time while the B.D. part is permutated by sixteenths.

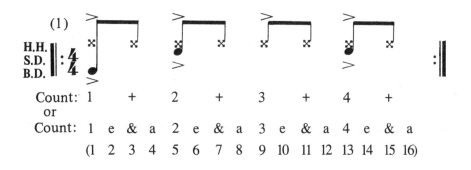

Even though the pattern is eighth notes, the counting can be done by sixteenths because the B.D. part will be permutating by sixteenths. To get exercise 2, move only the B.D. part to the right by one sixteenth note. The hand part remains the same, while the B.D. moves to the right by sixteenth notes.

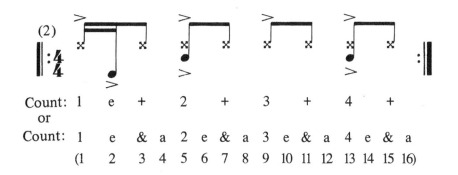

The same process is repeated in exercises 3–16 until the B.D. part has moved through all the available sixteenth notes. There are a total of 16 exercises because of the 16 sixteenth notes in a bar of 4/4. In each study, as the stickings and accents shift in relation to the quarter note, notice how different each exercise sounds in comparison to its beginning exercise. Counting aloud through each exercise will help you to better hear how these rhythms are moving across each quarter note. This habit is a very important key in building and establishing a strong "groove" sense. This key becomes of even greater importance as the studies become more complex. Permutation can be applied successfully to most rhythmic patterns. Don't forget to pay *close* attention to the accented and unaccented notes (for a detailed explanation of the accented-, unaccented-note concept, refer to "Development of the Two Sound-Levels with the Hands," page 7).

22

PERMUTATION STUDY #1

In studies #1–8, play each exercise at least eight times,
then proceed to the next exercise without stopping.

B.D. moves to the right one sixteenth note in each measure.

Repeat the entire page, changing the
eighth-note pattern on the H.H. to hand-
to-hand sixteenths on the H.H. and S.D.

PERMUTATION STUDY #2

PERMUTATION STUDY #3

This study uses the same H.H., B.D. and accented S.D. parts as in Study #2, with the addition of unaccented S.D. notes that outline the H.H., B.D. and accented S.D. to produce continuous sixteenth notes. In exercises 2, 8, 10 and 16, the S.D. is omitted in the places where the B.D. plays.

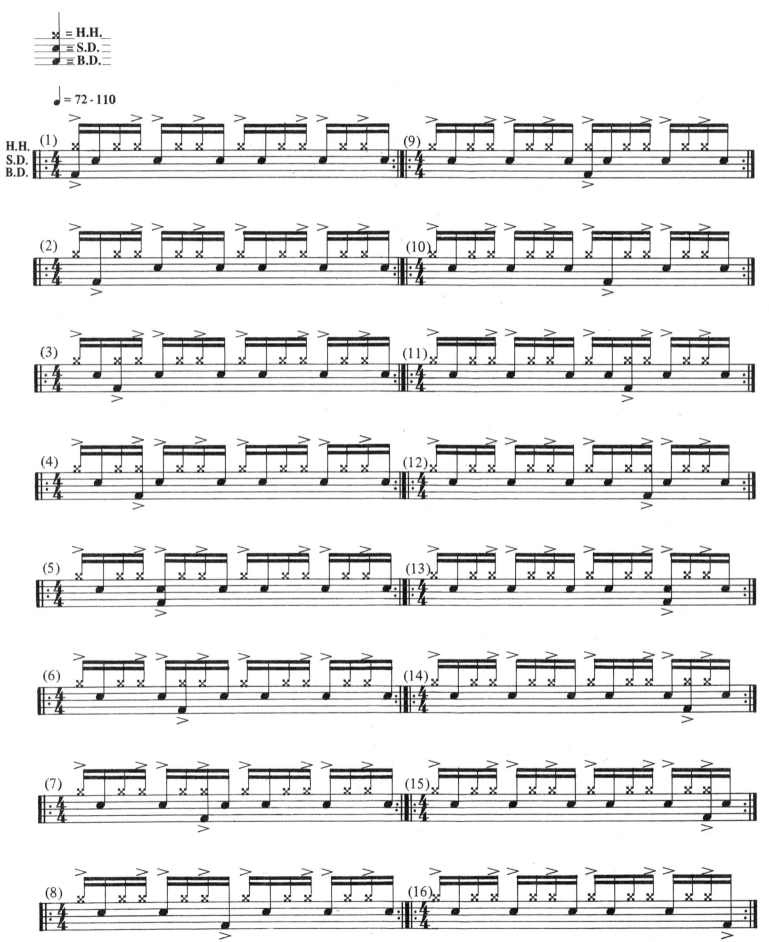

PERMUTATION STUDY #4

In the numbered column, the H.H. part is eighth notes. In the lettered column, the H.H. part includes sixteenth notes—same S.D. part with B.D. permutations throughout.

Accent S.D.

Accent S.D.

Accent S.D.

Accent S.D.

Permutation Study #4 (continued)

Accent S.D. — (10)

Accent S.D. — (10)

Accent S.D. — (12)

Accent S.D. — (12)

Accent S.D. — (13)

Accent S.D. — (13)

Accent S.D. — (15)

Accent S.D. — (15)

PERMUTATION STUDY #5

In this study the H.H. part is the same as in Study #4. The B.D. permutates and the unaccented S.D. outlines each exercise to produce continuous sixteenth notes.

PERMUTATION STUDY #6

Studies #6–8 go together and demonstrate three different ways to play the same rhythm.

In Study #6, only the B.D. part permutates, while the H.H. and accented S.D. remain the same throughout.

In Study #7, the H.H. and accented S.D. are the same as in Study #6, while the unaccented S.D. outlines the same B.D. part as it permutates.

In Study #8, the accented S.D. is the same as in Studies #6 and #7. The H.H. part is broken up and helps the unaccented S.D. outline the same B.D. part as it permutates.

PERMUTATION STUDY #7

PERMUTATION STUDY #8

PERMUTATION STUDY #9

Because this is a two-beat rhythm in a bar of 4/4, it will only permutate eight times. The right hand plays the H.H., while the left hand plays the S.D. and toms. The hands can be reversed, with the left hand playing the H.H. and the right hand playing the S.D. and toms.

Play either one of these time patterns before each exercise:

This study can be performed with the hands reversed. Play the time pattern with R.H./H.H., L.H./S.D.

PERMUTATION STUDY #10

The H.H., B.D. and S.D. parts all permutate in this study.

Time Pattern: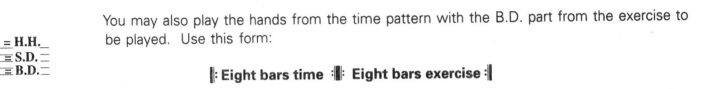

You may also play the hands from the time pattern with the B.D. part from the exercise to be played. Use this form:

‖: Eight bars time :‖: Eight bars exercise :‖

♩ = 72 - 104

PERMUTATION STUDY #11

This study uses all four limbs —H.H., B.D., S.D. and L.F./H.H. All parts permutate by sixteenth notes.

PERMUTATION STUDY #12

In exercises 1–16, the R.H. plays the S.D. and toms, while the L.H. plays the H.H. The H.H., S.D., B.D. and toms permutate in each exercise.

Play this pattern before exercises 1–16.

Notice that in the time pattern the R.H. plays the H.H. and the L.H. plays the S.D., while in the exercises the R.H. plays the S.D. and toms.

Play this pattern before exercises 17–32.

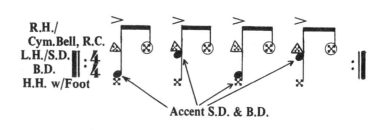

Accent S.D. & B.D.

Cym.Bell

Accent B.D.

F R L R L R R F R L R L R R L R

In exercises 17–32, the R.H. plays cowbell or the cymbal bell, while the L.H. plays the S.D. and toms. The cowbell/cymbal, S.D., toms and B.D. permutate while the H.H. plays quarter notes in each exercise. (Same permutations as exercises 1–16.)

PERMUTATION STUDY #13

Permutation Studies #13–16 permutate by eighth notes.

Open = ○
Closed = +
H.H. =
S.D. =
B.D. =
H.H. = w/Foot

♩ = 90-112

Play this pattern before each exercise in studies #13–15:

Use this form: ‖: Eight bars time :‖: Eight bars exercise :‖

36

Permutation Study #14

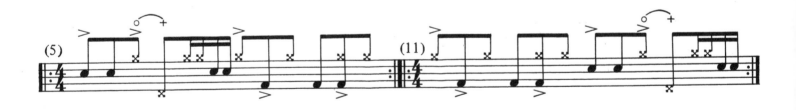

PERMUTATION STUDY #15

PERMUTATION STUDY #16

PERMUTATION STUDY #17

Time Pattern:

Use this form: ‖: **Eight bars time** :‖: **Eight bars exercise** :‖

*When going back to time pattern, omit the B.D. on beat one, bar one only.

GROOVE STUDIES

Groove studies are exercises built upon the concept of playing consistent time that "feels good" while performing one or a series of hand/foot variations. The exercises vary in difficulty (from easy to difficult) and include many unusual ways of combining the hands and feet. Each study begins with an exercise that is the basic theme of that study. The exercises that follow are variations on the beginning exercise.

When performing the individual studies, play each exercise for 4, 8 or 16 measures, then without stopping, proceed to the next one in or out of sequence. To build endurance, play each exercise for five minutes, and without stopping, proceed to the next one in or out of sequence. Obviously, with the number of exercises in each study, performing them this way would be very time consuming. Try any group of four exercises for a 20-minute workout. To build relaxation into this routine, stop at the first signs of tension and begin again.

All the exercises throughout this book combine technique with a musical idea. The performance of this material includes repetition, which builds technique, concentration, endurance, etc. Get in the habit of playing with the same conviction that you would if you were playing in a real musical situation with other players. Once this is done and you are familiar enough with the material, get together with some rhythm section players and build music around these grooves, as well as some of your own. See pages 18–20 for additional practice/performance techniques. Keep in mind that the metronome markings are only suggested markings. Play each study at a tempo within your physical capabilities, advancing the metronome as you gain control of each series of exercises.

GROOVE STUDY #1

GROOVE STUDY #2

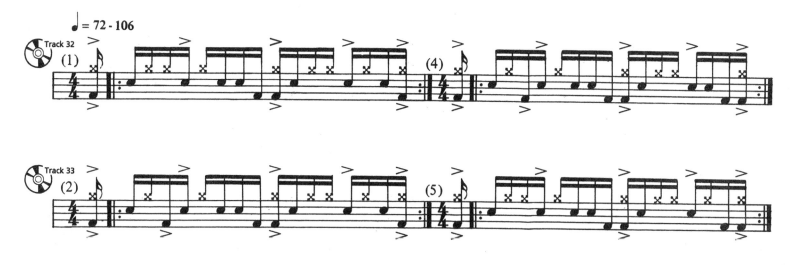

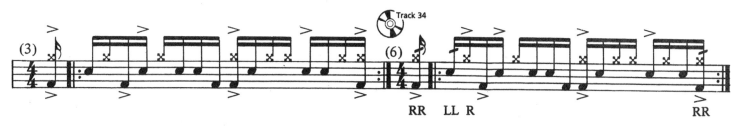

GROOVE STUDY #3

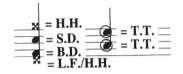

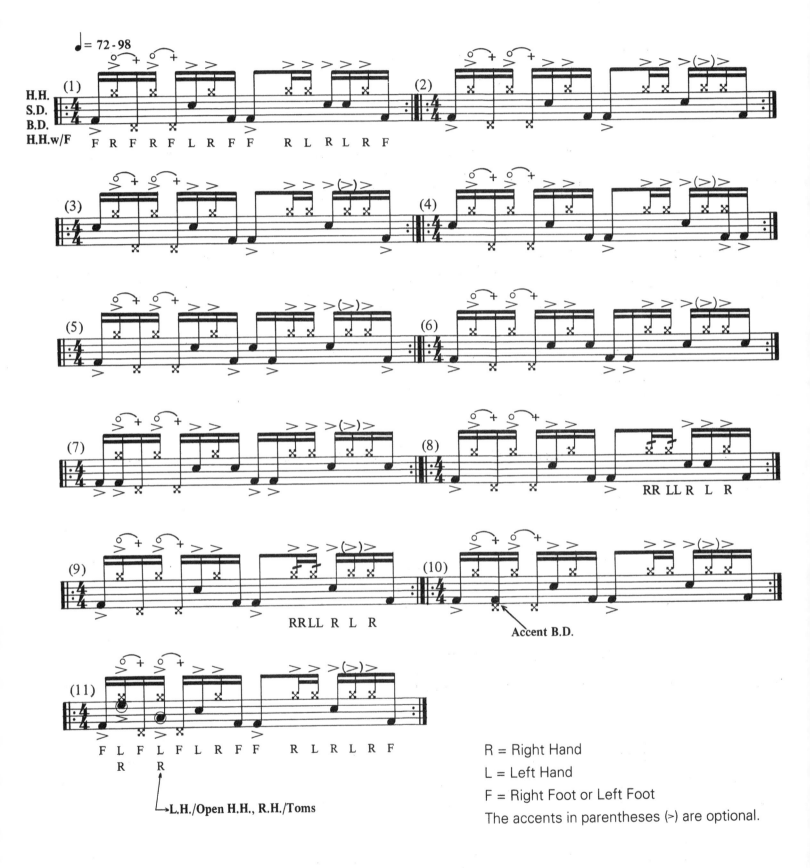

R = Right Hand
L = Left Hand
F = Right Foot or Left Foot
The accents in parentheses (>) are optional.

Be sure to watch the sticking throughout that is given in exercise 1, with the exception of exercise 11.

GROOVE STUDY #4

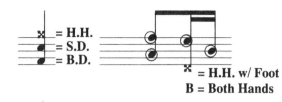

♩ = 72 - 92

GROOVE STUDY #4 (continued)

F F R L F R F F   B

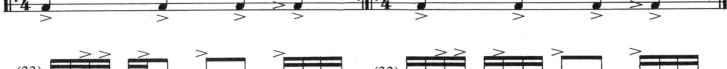

GROOVE STUDY #5

This study is a series of six, four-measure exercises. Measure 1 in each exercise is different; measures 2–4 in each exercise are the same. Measures 2 and 3 are single paradiddles (RLRR LRLL), while measure 4 is built upon the paradiddle-diddle (RLRRLL). It is important to observe that any notes or accents in parentheses are to be omitted when the exercises repeat. For example, in exercise 1, the accent and B.D. on beat one are in parentheses, so they would be omitted when the exercise repeats. This is also true when proceeding directly, without stopping, from one exercise to the next where parentheses are indicated. If exercises are played individually, then the only time the parentheses are not observed is on the initial downbeat leaving only an unaccented H.H. to be played on beat one. The same is seen in exercises 2 and 3. Measure 4 of each exercise is very important—please note the sticking and the cymbal crashes.

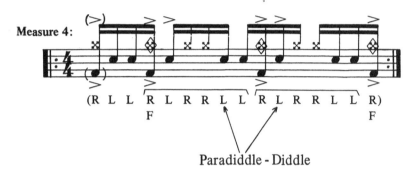

After working out this measure, go to exercise 1 and put together the transition from measure 4 back to measure 1. Notice the effect that omitting the notes and accents in parentheses has when making this transition.

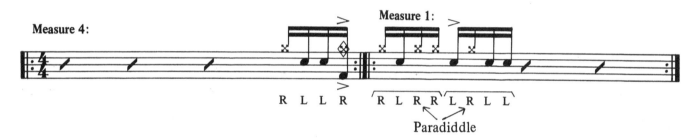

Next, work out measure 1 of the remaining exercises, making sure to understand the differences in each. Be able to play each one comfortably. These measures work well as separate grooves and can be played as such. Finally, put each exercise together, performing each separately until comfortable. You may also play the entire study from top to bottom without stopping. Play each exercise at least four times before proceeding to the next. The exercises can be performed in or out of sequence.

GROOVE STUDY #5 (continued)

GROOVE STUDY #6

GROOVE STUDY #7

RR LL F

50

GROOVE STUDY #8

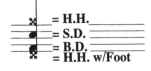

= H.H.
= S.D.
= B.D.
= H.H. w/Foot

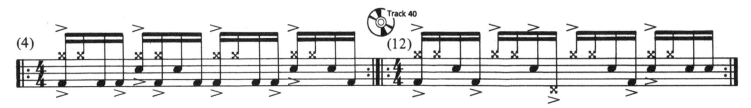

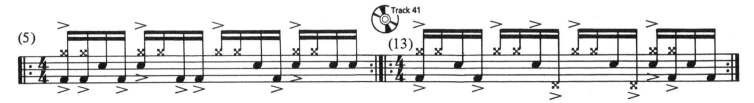

51

GROOVE STUDY #8 (continued)

GROOVE STUDY #9

GROOVE STUDY #10

Groove Study #11

Most drummers playing a right-handed drum set have the hi-hat positioned on the left side of the kit and they play the H.H. with the right hand. These exercises use an additional closed hi-hat placed somewhere on the right side of the drum set. The right hi-hat is notated R.H.H. and is to be played with the right hand. The left hi-hat is notated L.H.H. and is played with the left hand. The stickings are notated under each exercise.

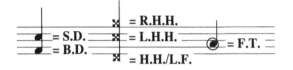

L R R L R L L F R L R R L R F R

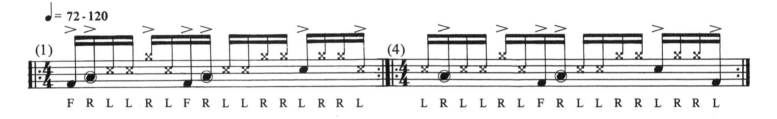

(1) F R L L R L F R L L R R L R R L   (4) L R L L R L F R L L R R L R R L

(2) F R L L R L R L L R L F L R R L   (5) L R L L R L F R L L R R L R L F

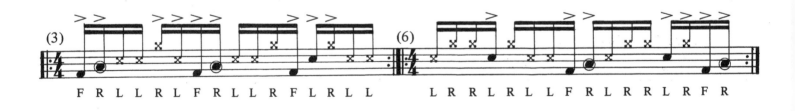

(3) F R L L R L F R L L R F L R L L   (6) L R R L R L L F R L R R L R F R

GROOVE STUDY #12

GROOVE STUDY #13

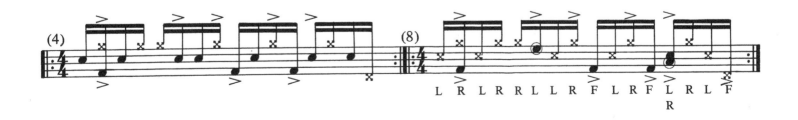

GROOVE STUDY #14

Watch for the exercises using two hi-hats.

Accent S.D.

GROOVE STUDY #14 (continued)

Accent S.D.

GROOVE STUDY #14 (continued)

The *unaccented* notes are *cymbal*, the *accented* notes are *cymbal bell*.

GROOVE STUDY #14 (continued)

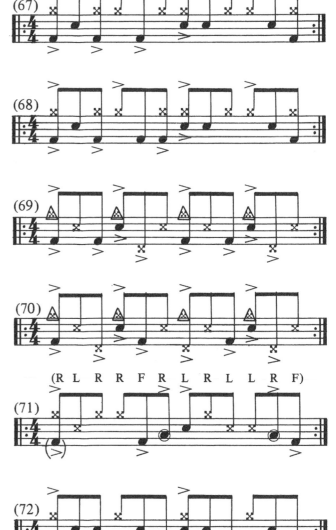

GROOVE STUDY #15

In exercises 7 and 8, the R.H./H.H. becomes R.H./Cym. and T.T. The R.H. plays back and forth between the ride cymbal and tom. The L.H. stays on the closed H.H. (In exercise 8, accent the H.H. on 2 and 4, just like the H.H. pattern in exercise 7.)

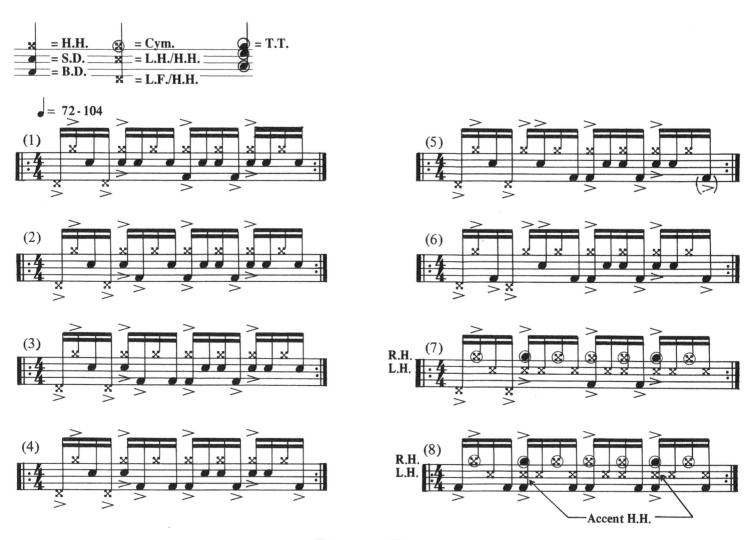

RANDOM IDEAS

Random Ideas are a collection of beats. Some are individual grooves, while others are in groups of two, three or four ideas that go together. All can be developed even further by substituting one voice for another (for example: L.F./H.H. for B.D. or vice versa; T.T. for S.D.; C.B. for H.H.) and/or using the permutation concept.

The L.H. plays the left cymbal bell.
The R.H. plays H.H. and S.D.

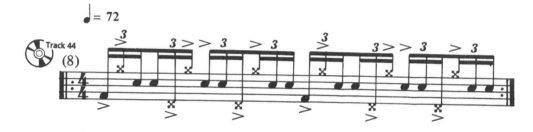

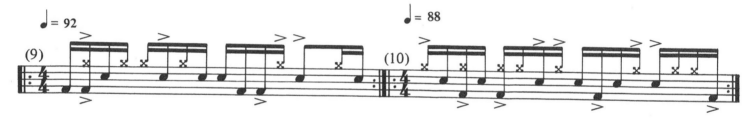

#13 The C.B. is positioned on the ride side of the set. The C.B. and F.T. are played with the right hand. The H.H., S.D. and T.T. are played with the left hand.

Exercises 15 and 16 begin with the sixteenth that's written outside of the repeat sign.

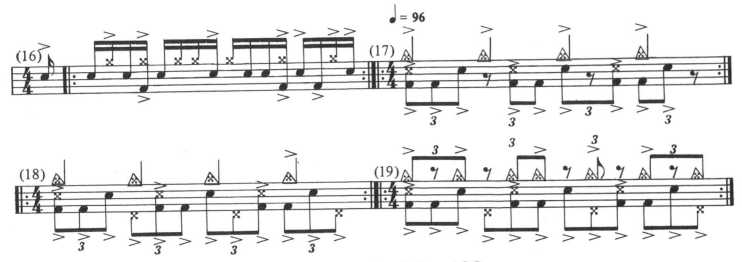

#18 The R.H. plays quarter notes on cym. bell; the L.H. plays H.H. and S.D.

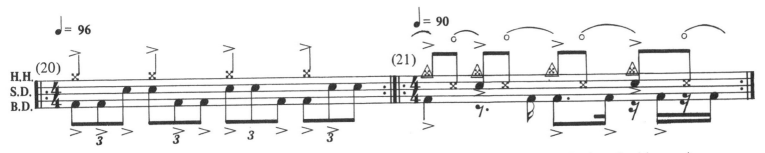

#21 The R.H. plays the cym. bell; the L.H. plays open H.H. and S.D. (The H.H. doesn't close in this one.)

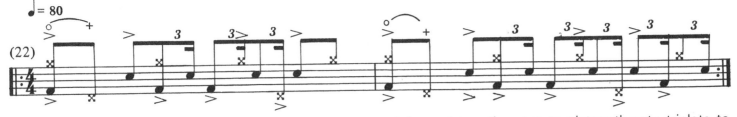

A great deal of the material in this book can be converted from sixteenth notes to sixteenth-note triplets to produce a shuffle sound.

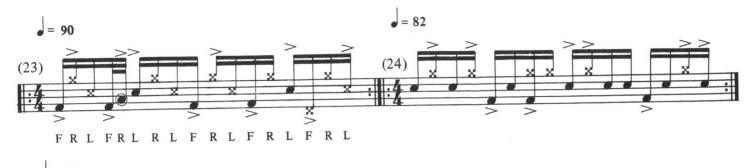

F R L   F R L   R L   F   R L   F R L   F R L

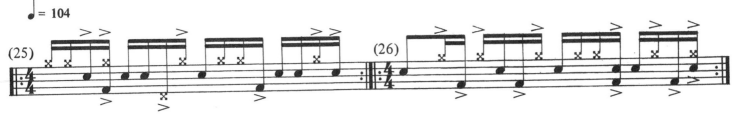

♩ = 95

(27)

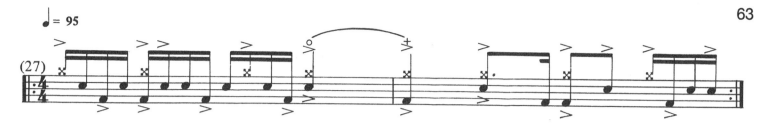

♩ = 90

(28) (29)

♩ = 102

(30) (31)

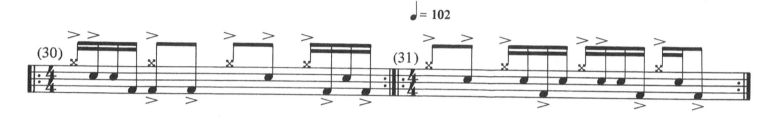

(32)

♩ = 86

(33) (34)

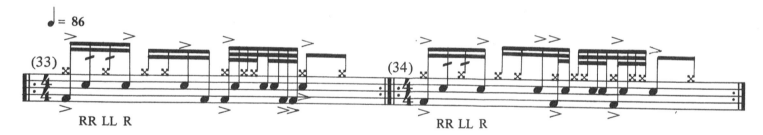

RR LL R   RR LL R

♩ = 108   ♩ = 108

R.H.H. (35)   L.H.H. (36)

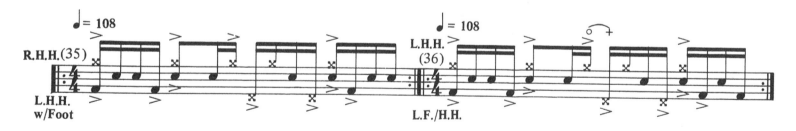

L.H.H. w/Foot   L.F./H.H.

♩ = 117

(37)

♩ = 114

(38)

64

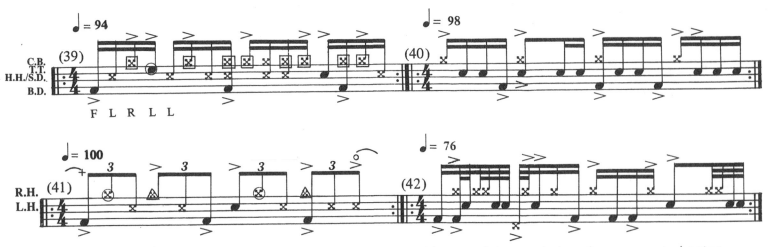

F L R L L

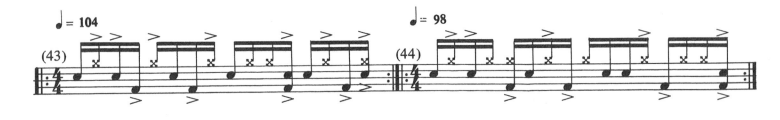

#41 The R.H. plays the cym. bell on the accented notes, the ride part of the cymbal on the unaccented notes.

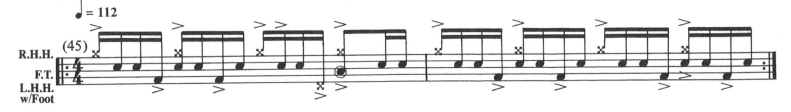

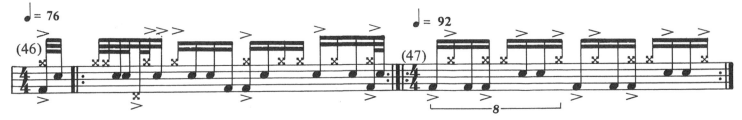

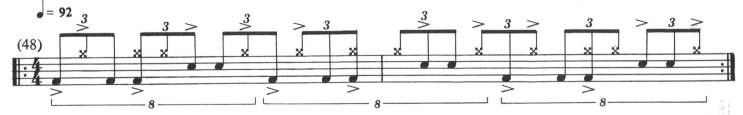

#48 This eight-note sticking is the same as in #47 except it's being played as eighth-note triplets.

CONTENTS

SCOTT JOPLIN
ARRANGED BY LAWRENCE ROSEN

18 RAGS
IN EASIER VERSIONS

ED 4099

ISBN 978-0-7935-4621-3

G. SCHIRMER, Inc.
DISTRIBUTED BY

HAL•LEONARD®
CORPORATION
7777 W. BLUEMOUND RD. P.O. BOX 13819 MILWAUKEE, WI 53213

ALL IS FOUND

Music and Lyrics by KRISTEN ANDERSON-LOPEZ
and ROBERT LOPEZ

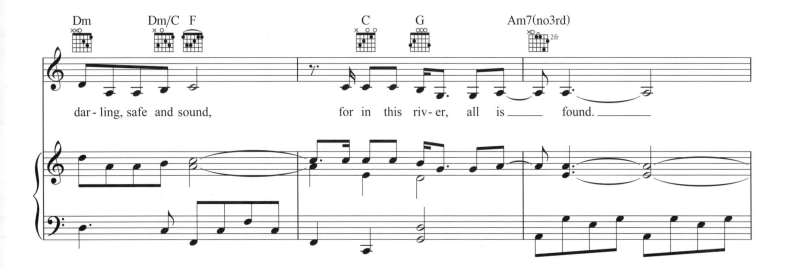

SOME THINGS NEVER CHANGE

Music and Lyrics by KRISTEN ANDERSON-LOPEZ
and ROBERT LOPEZ

Pump-kin just be-came fer-ti-liz - er.

OLAF: And my leaf's a lit-tle sad-der and wis - er.

ANNA: That's why I __

__ re - ly __ on cer-tain cer - tain - ties. Yes,

Swing 16ths

some things nev - er change, __ like the feel of your hand __ in mine. __

Some things stay the same, __ like how we get a - long __ just fine. __ Like an old __

OLAF: like how we get a - long __ just fine. __

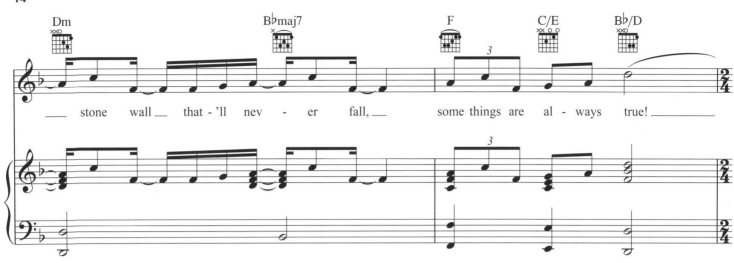

stone wall ___ that-'ll nev - er fall, ___ some things are al - ways true! ___

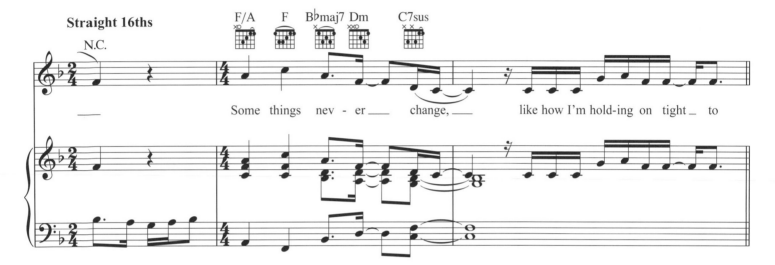

Straight 16ths

Some things nev - er ___ change, ___ like how I'm hold-ing on tight ___ to

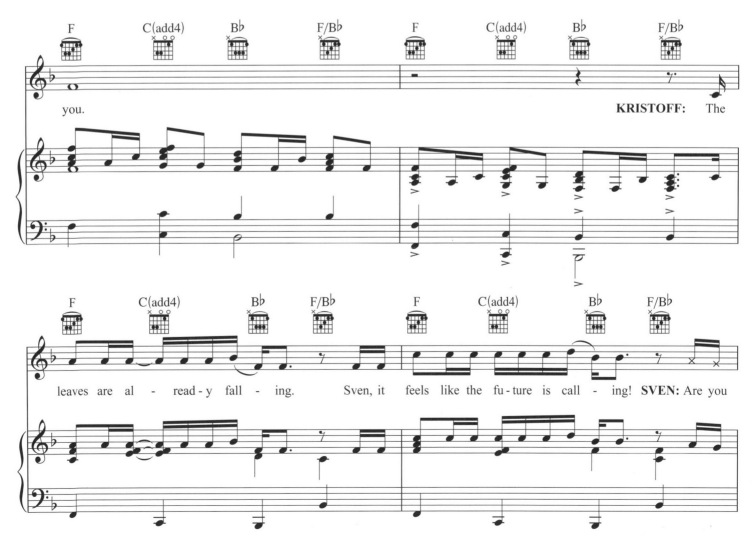

you.

KRISTOFF: The

leaves are al - read-y fall - ing. Sven, it feels like the fu - ture is call - ing! SVEN: Are you

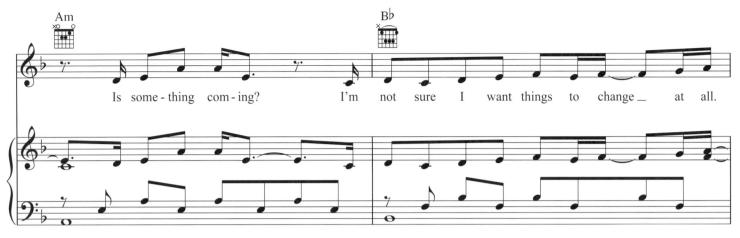

Is some-thing com-ing? I'm not sure I want things to change __ at all.

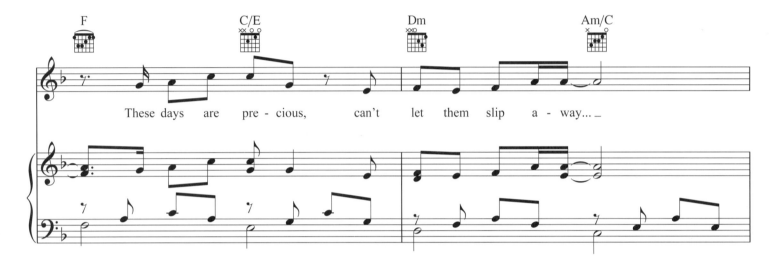

These days are pre-cious, can't let them slip a-way... __

I can't freeze this mo-ment, but I can still go out __ and seize this __

__ day!! __

REINDEER(S) ARE BETTER THAN PEOPLE (CONT.)

Music and Lyrics by KRISTEN ANDERSON-LOPEZ
and ROBERT LOPEZ

INTO THE UNKNOWN

Music and Lyrics by KRISTEN ANDERSON-LOPEZ
and ROBERT LOPEZ

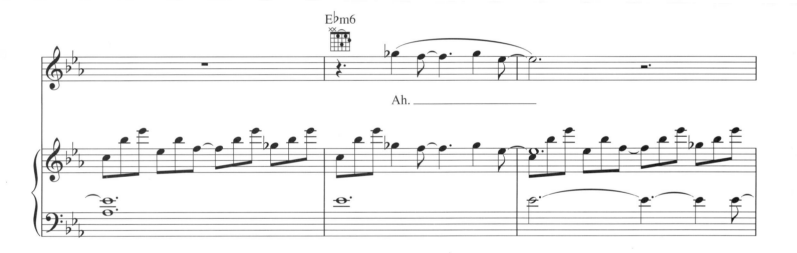

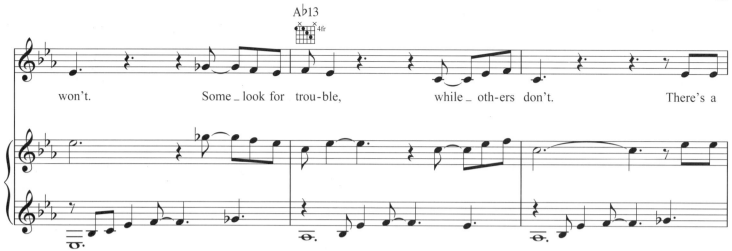

won't. Some_ look for trou-ble, while_ oth-ers don't. There's a

thou - sand rea - sons ___ I should go a-bout my day ___ and ig-

nore your whis - pers, ___ which I wish would go a - way... _____ Oh. ____

___ (Ah. _____ Oh. _____ Ah.) _____

24

With determination

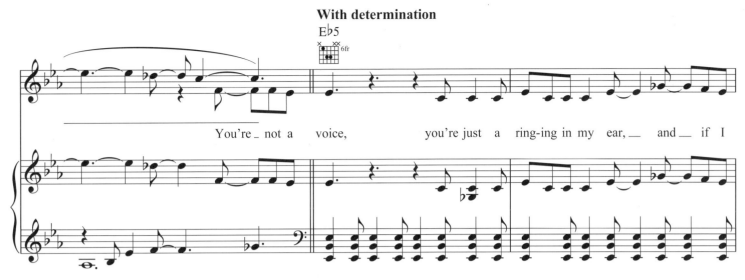

You're _ not a voice, you're just a ring-ing in my ear, _ and _ if I

heard you, _ which I don't, I'm spo-ken for, _ I _ fear.

Ev-'ry-one I've ev-er loved is here with-in these walls. _ I'm

sor-ry, se-cret si-ren, but I'm block-ing out your calls. _ I've

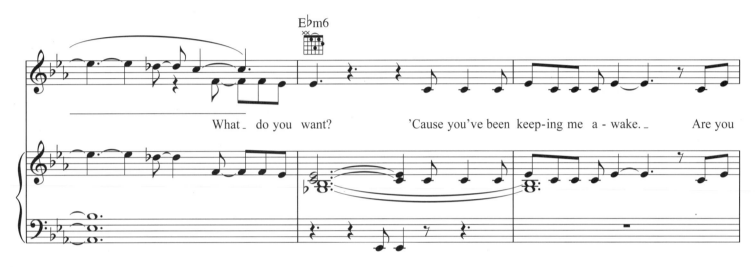

What _ do you want? 'Cause you've been keep-ing me a - wake. _ Are you

here _____ to dis - tract me so I make a big mis - take? _

Slower, with freedom

Or are you some - one out there who's a lit - tle bit like me? _ Who

knows deep down I'm not where I'm meant to be? __ Ev - 'ry

Driving

day's a lit - tle hard - er as I feel my pow - er grow! __

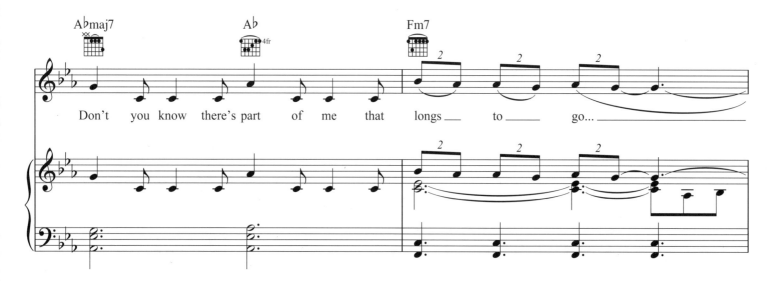

Don't you know there's part of me that longs __ to __ go... __

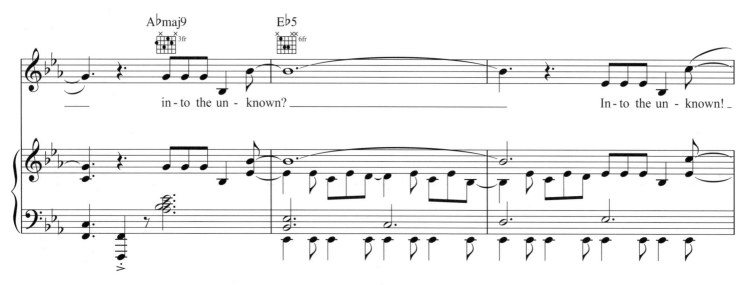

__ in - to the un - known? __ In - to the un - known! _

WHEN I AM OLDER

Music and Lyrics by KRISTEN ANDERSON-LOPEZ
and ROBERT LOPEZ

OLAF: *What was that?!* *Samantha?*

This will all make sense when I am old - er.

Some-day, I will see that this makes sense. One day, __ when I'm old and wise, __

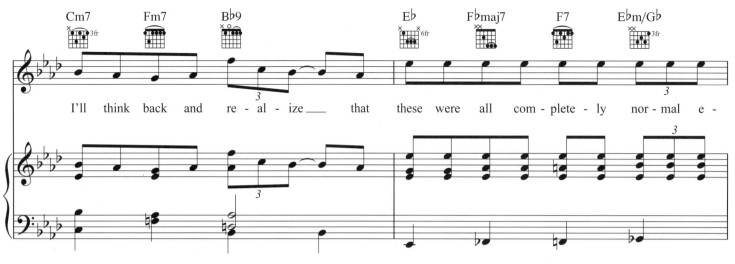

I'll think back and re-al-ize___ that these were all com-plete-ly nor-mal e-

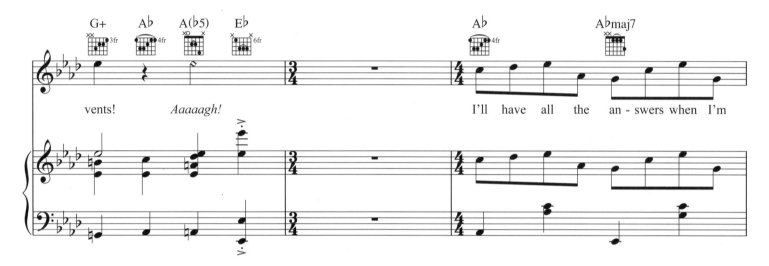

vents! *Aaaaagh!* I'll have all the an-swers when I'm

old-er! Like, why we're in this dark, en-chant-ed wood.

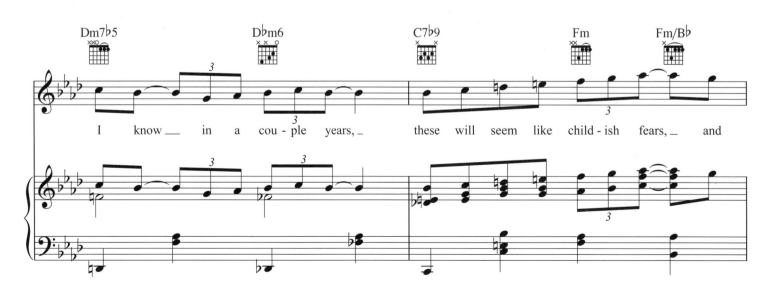

I know___ in a cou-ple years, _ these will seem like child-ish fears, _ and

LOST IN THE WOODS

Music and Lyrics by KRISTEN ANDERSON-LOPEZ
and ROBERT LOPEZ

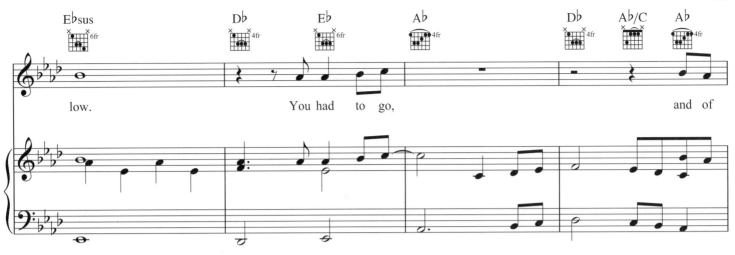

low. You had to go, and of

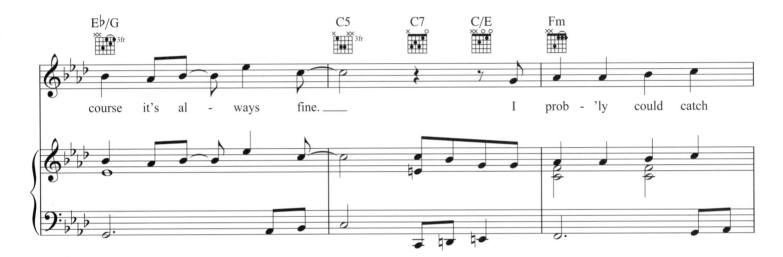

course it's al - ways fine. ___ I prob - 'ly could catch

up with you to - mor - row. ___ But is

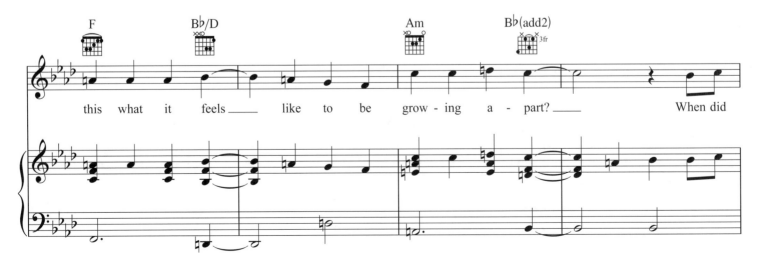

this what it feels ___ like to be grow - ing a - part? ___ When did

I be-come the one ___ who's al-ways chas-ing your heart? ___ Now I

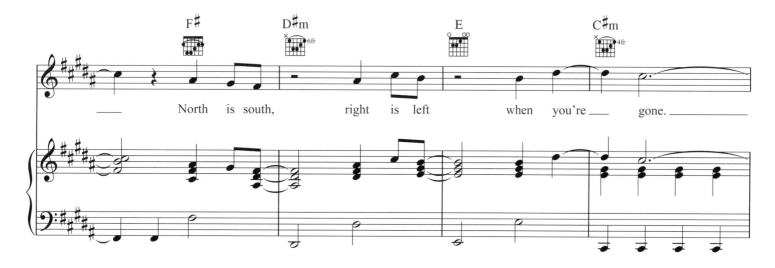

turn a-round ___ and find I am lost in the woods. ___

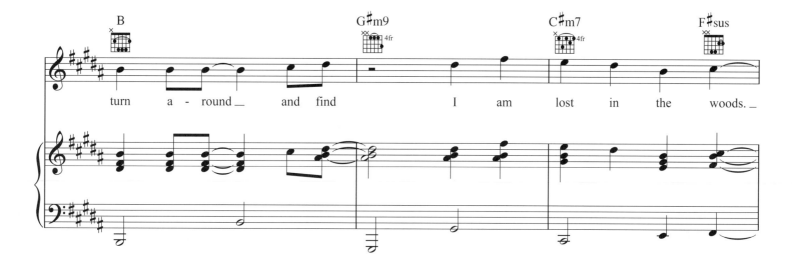

___ North is south, right is left when you're ___ gone. ___

___ I'm the one ___ who sees you home, but now I'm lost in the woods, ___

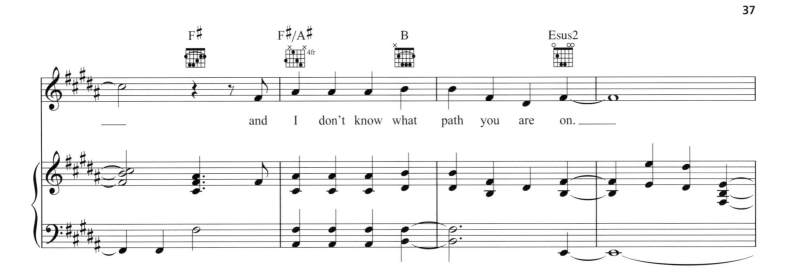

and I don't know what path you are on. ____

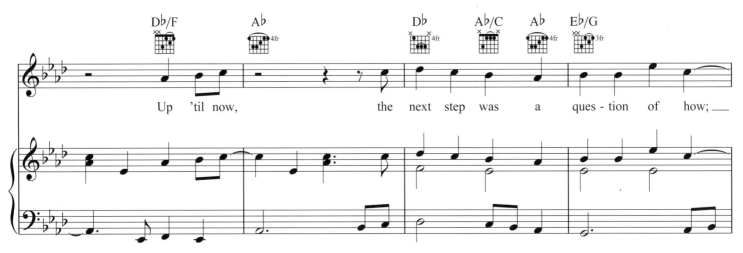

I'm lost in the woods. ____

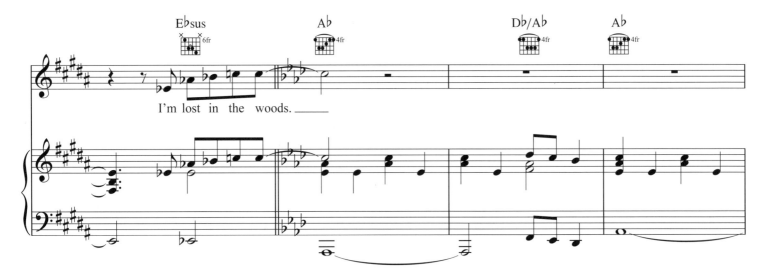

Up 'til now, the next step was a ques-tion of how; ____

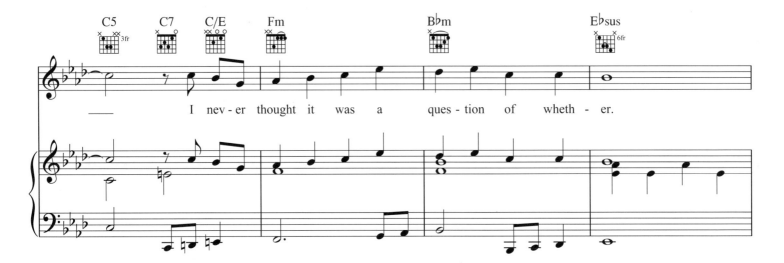

____ I nev-er thought it was a ques-tion of wheth-er.

Who am I _____ if I'm not your guy? _____

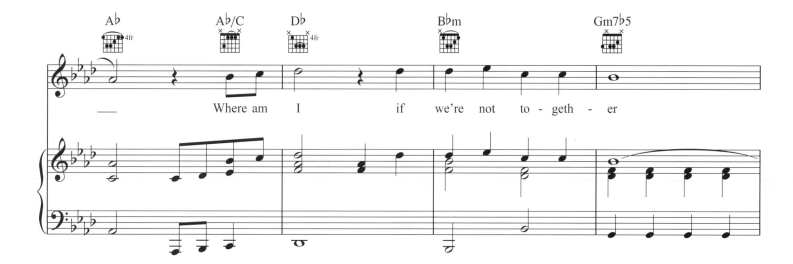

_____ Where am I if we're not to - geth - er

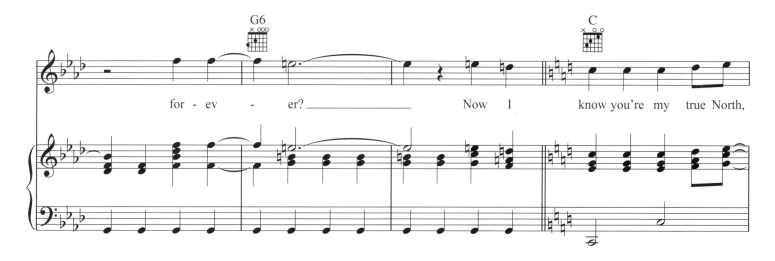

for - ev - er? _____ Now I know you're my true North,

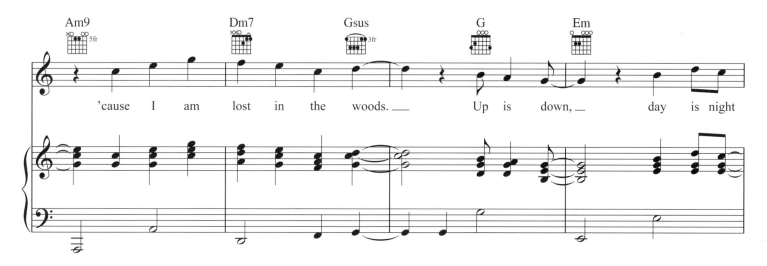

'cause I am lost in the woods. _____ Up is down, _____ day is night

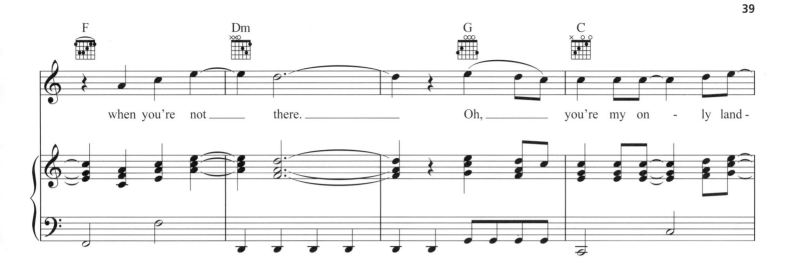

when you're not _____ there. _____ Oh, _____ you're my on - ly land -

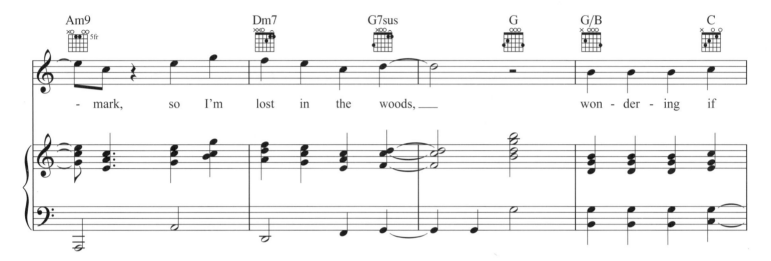

- mark, so I'm lost in the woods, ___ won - der - ing if

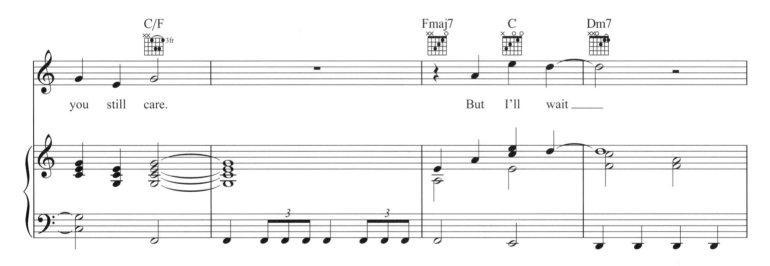

you still care. But I'll wait _____

for a sign ___ that I'm ___ your _____ path,

'cause you ___ are mine. Un - til then, I'm

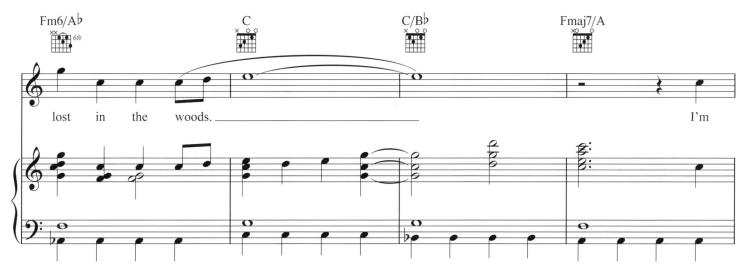

lost in the woods. _____ I'm

lost in the woods. _____ I'm

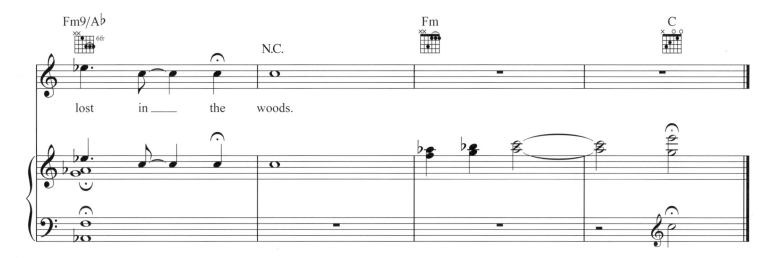

lost in ___ the woods.

SHOW YOURSELF

Music and Lyrics by KRISTEN ANDERSON-LOPEZ
and ROBERT LOPEZ

like a friend I've al - ways known. _____ I'm ar-

riv - ing, and it feels like I am home. _____ I have

C#(add4)   C#/B   B

al - ways been ____ a for - tress, cold se - crets deep __ in - side. ____

B(add4)/A   A   A/D   D

You have se - crets too, ____ but you don't have __ to

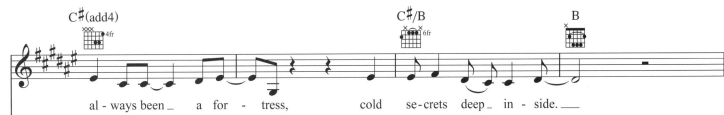

riv - er _____ full of mem-o - ry.) _____ **IDUNA:** Come, my dar - ling, home - ward _

_ bound. _____ I am found!
ELSA:

ELSA/IDUNA: Show your - self! _

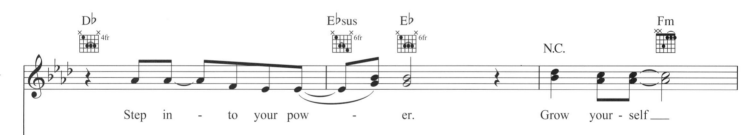

Step in - to your pow - er. Grow your - self _

in - to some - thing new. **IDUNA:** (You are the one _ you've been wait -

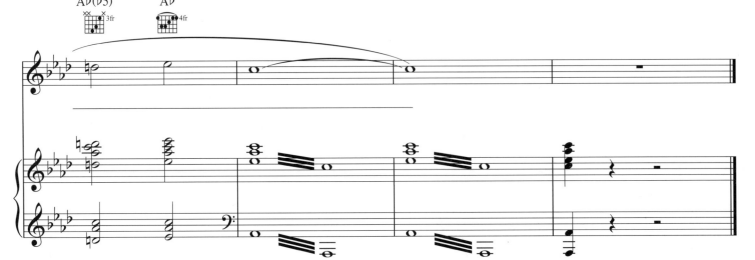

THE NEXT RIGHT THING

Music and Lyrics by KRISTEN ANDERSON-LOPEZ
and ROBERT LOPEZ

Moderately slow, with freedom

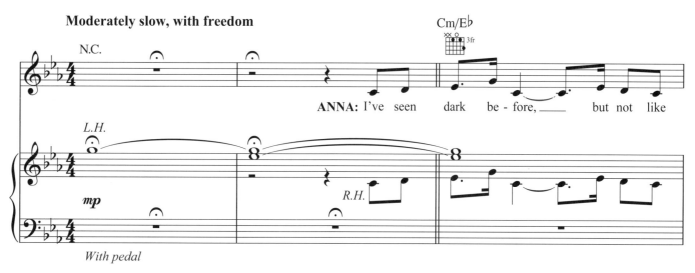

ANNA: I've seen dark be - fore, _____ but not like

this; this is cold, this is emp - ty, this is numb. The

life I knew is o - ver; _ the lights are out. Hel - lo dark - ness, _ I'm read - y to suc-

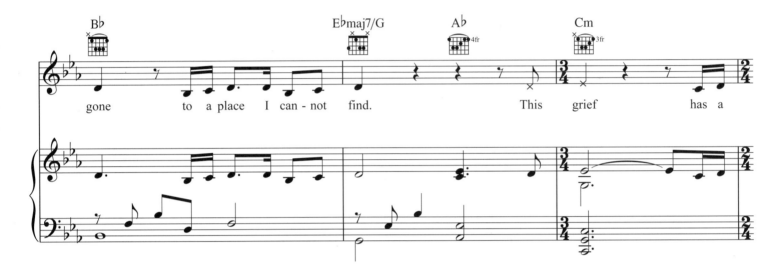

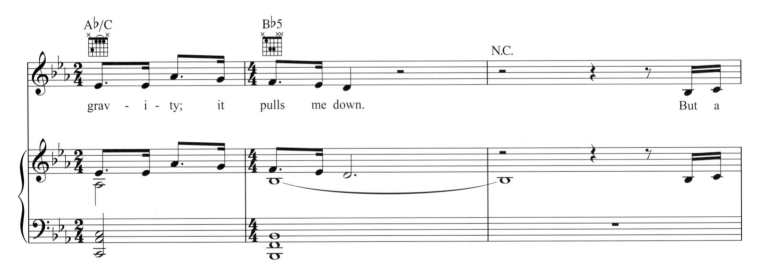

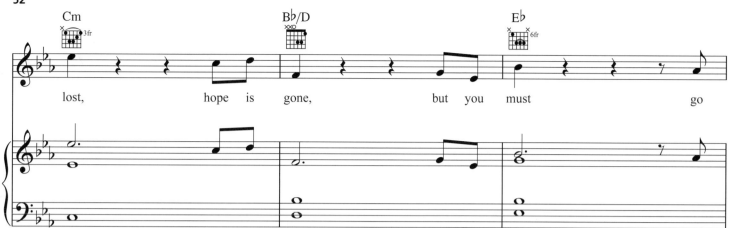

lost, hope is gone, but you must go

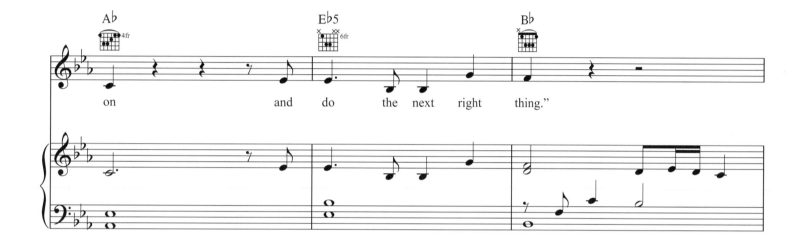

on and do the next right thing."

Steadily

N.C.

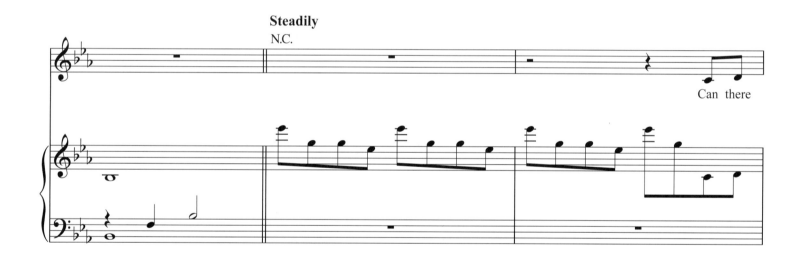

Can there

be a day be-yond this night? I don't know _ an-y-more _ what is true. _

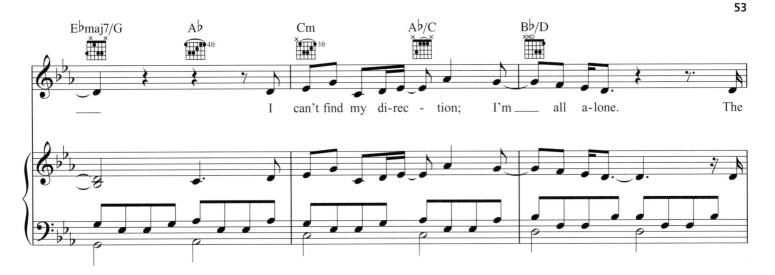

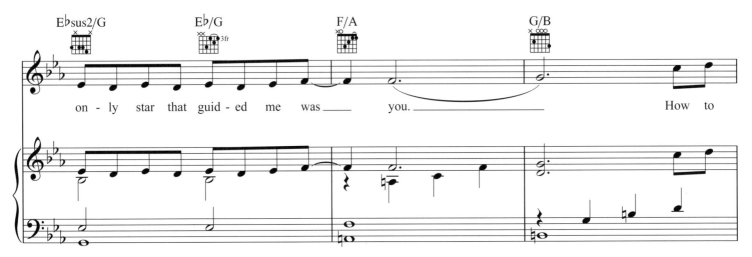

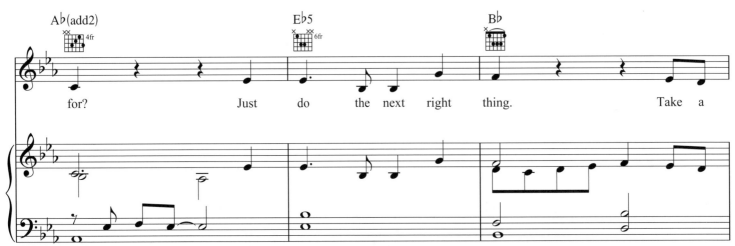

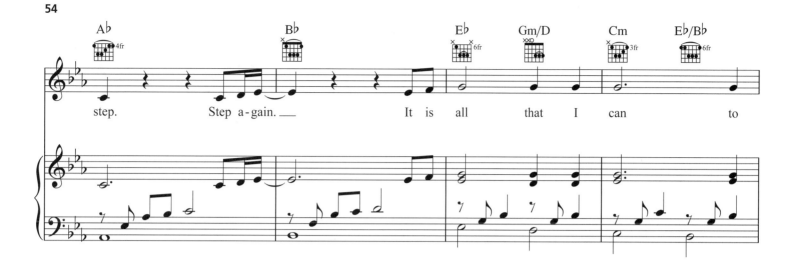

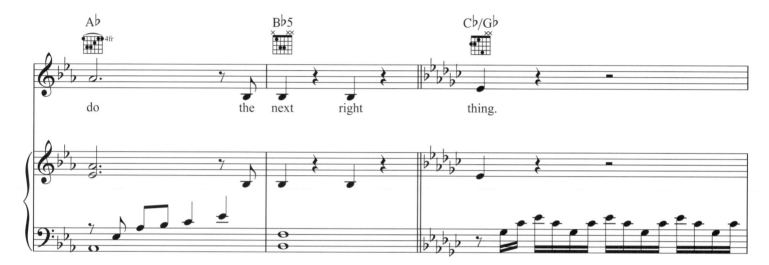

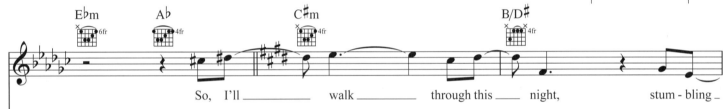

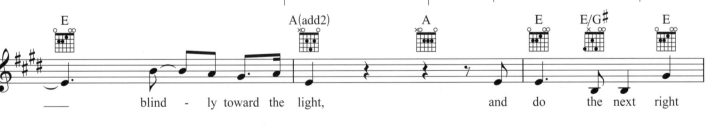